River *of* Words

Selected by Robert Hass

**Annual Poetry & Art Contest
On the Theme of Watersheds
2000 Winning Poems**

A Project of
International Rivers Network
&
The Library of Congress
Center for the Book

Copyright © 2000 River of Words Project™
For more information or to order additional copies of this
book, the River of Words Teacher's Guide, art notecards,
t-shirts, or other materials, contact:

> The River of Words Project™
> P.O. Box 4000-J
> Berkeley, CA 94704
> Tel: 510-433-7020 • Fax: 510-848-1008
> Email: row@irn.org • Website: http://www.riverofwords.org

Printed in the United States of America by West Coast Print Center
ISSN: 1529-2533
ISBN: 0-9662771-4-7

River of Words ROWing Partners—

The following organizations and individuals have made substantial contributions to River of Words:

American Booksellers Association
Anacostia Watershed Society
Blue Fish Clothing
The Center for Ecoliteracy
Geraldine R. Dodge Foundation
Lannan Foundation
Library of America

Magnetic Poetry
Northern California
    Environmental Grantmakers
The Rhode Island Foundation
The Slide Factory
Tony Spiers
The Windfall Foundation
West Coast Print Center

River of Words Staff
Pamela Michael, Director
Shannon Wilson, Project Assistant
Lorena Cassady, Contest Assistant
Aleta George, Contest Assistant

River of Words Volunteers
Belle Kevin
Betty Ann Webster
Zola de Firmian

Design by Zola de Firmian

River of Words™ is an international literacy and arts education project designed to nurture respect and understanding of the natural world. Children are encouraged to learn their "ecological address" and to describe through poetry and art their own "place in space." The project hopes to foster responsibility, imagination and action in young people and to publicly acknowledge their creativity and concerns. It is co-sponsored by International Rivers Network, The Library of Congress Center for the Book and United States Poet Laureate (1995-1997) Robert Hass.

Thousands of schoolchildren in kindergarten though 12th grade have participated in our annual River of Words Contest drawn by the challenge of exploring and interpreting their local watersheds through the arts. The project employs a variety of classroom and field activities, all explained to teachers in a curriculum guide distributed to schools, libraries, nature centers, bookstores and youth organizations.

Each year national Grand Prize winners (four in poetry and four in art) and one international winner are chosen to go to Washington, DC with their parents where they are honored at an award ceremony, luncheon, public reading and art show at The Library of Congress. River of Words also honors a "Teacher of the Year" and a San Francisco Bay Area and a Washington, DC Area winner annually.

International Rivers Network (IRN) is a non-profit organization dedicated to protecting and preserving the world's rivers and the rights of the people who depend on them.

The Library of Congress Center for the Book was established by an Act of Congress in 1977 to foster understanding of the vital role of books, reading, libraries, and literacy in society.

About This Book—

A recent study showed that while children in the United States could identify over a thousand corporate logos, few could recognize and name more than a handful of the plants that grew in their own neighborhoods. As a nation we have—within our lifetimes—lost our understanding of the natural world, and our sense of connection and belonging to a particular place. This fragmentation of landscapes and cultural threads is being repeated throughout the world. River of Words was created to help children regain an intimacy with the web of life and to develop a rich and sustaining "language of landscape."

The careful articulation of the natural world that the River of Words multidisciplinary "Watershed Explorer" curriculum encourages, and the metaphors that these young explorers create from their meticulous observations, all serve to clarify scientific phenomena and to connect students to their surroundings in very profound ways. By studying their particular watershed and the art, music and literature it has inspired, students can discover their place in a wider community and learn about their geographical history, weather patterns, flora and fauna, indigenous cultural traditions, as well as the history of local migration and commerce. It is our hope that the structured, yet endlessly adaptive, exploration model that River of Words offers will lead young people to develop an abiding sense of belonging to a particular place—one that will someday guide them as informed and involved citizens.

The success of our free annual contest—its effectiveness in encouraging students to hone their powers of observation and expression—is due to creative local implementation of River of

Words by teachers, naturalists, youth counselors, museum docents and parents around the world. The poetry in this book is testament to the boundless skill, energy and love they bring to their work.

These poems are confirmation, too, of the curiosity, wisdom, caring, inventiveness, tender concerns and fierce commitment of today's youth. The winning poems have—from the beginning—been outstanding, but in the the first year or two many of the entries were either off-topic, formulaic or derivative. As students began to grasp the value of exploring and understanding their own neighborhoods and ecosystems, however—often through repeated visits to the same terrain—their language and images became more specific, richer, more startling and original.

So it is with great joy we offer these wonderful poems. Poetry and all the arts can teach us attention, help us fine tune our senses, draw us into relationship with the earth and with each other, and evoke our deepest emotions. In this way will watersheds and homegrounds be celebrated, revered, intimately understood, and ultimately preserved. Enjoy your swim in the "River of Words!"

Pamela Michael
River of Words Director and co-founder

TABLE OF CONTENTS

2000 RIVER OF WORDS GRAND PRIZES

Bugnibble *Calvin Hargis*	1
Swim In Me *Gracie Jordan*	2
Rockefeller Wildlife Preserve: Mid-August *Kevin Maher*	3
Dear Aquarius *Kt Harmon*	5

INTERNATIONAL GRAND PRIZE — 6
Untitled   *Christine Yin*

ANACOSTIA WATERSHED PRIZE — 8
Just Imagine   *El'Jay Johnson*

2000 RIVER OF WORDS FINALISTS

Nature's Notes *Amy Allred*	10
Snoqualmie River Flambé *Robin Andrews*	11
One with *Sable Aragon*	13
Eluding the Familiar *Anne Atwell-McLeod*	14
Water Shed Poem *Lucy Barber*	15
In Memorium *Alexis Kellner Becker*	16
Twilight *E.A. Blevins*	17
The Rain *Maddison Boewe*	18
First Winter's Fog *Margit Bowler*	19
The Storm Is Coming *Kevin Brown*	20
Snow *Chris Castillo*	20
Untitled *Josh Coomber*	21
Here is Life *Kelly Cox*	22
Untitled *Josh Davidson*	23
Water *Shawna Eiermann*	24
The Storm is Here *Miles Feld*	25

First Light *Graham Fischer-Corners*	26
Goldfish *Stefani Galik*	27
Mariquita / Ladybug *Yutzel Garcia*	28
a single drop *Emily Smith Gilbert*	29
Moon Song *Alice Goldfuss*	30
The Secret of the River *Joanna Laine Isaacs*	31
Virga *Mallory A. Jensen*	32
The Late Rose *Jane S. Jiang*	34
The River *John Keough*	35
Berry Falls *Malcolm Kim*	35
The Air *Emily Kirby*	36
Poseidon in the Infirmary *Anaïs Koivisto*	37
Wood of Feeling *Hannah Meade*	38
Deep Song of the River *Mod 1 Collaborative*	39
Wonder of Wonders *Ian Olsen*	40
Sunset *Daphne Payne*	41
Do You Hear It? *Tiffany Pope*	42
Woods Canyon Lake *Beth Prall*	43
The Rhythm of Life *Alicia D. Purdin*	44
The Millionth Circle *Leia Sandmann*	45
Mother of the Earth *Christie Swanson*	46
Elements *Marla Scott*	47
Shrimping *Amelia Sides*	48
The Clouds Are Once Again Too Big *Lyndsey Turner*	50
Tide / Gusts *Hans Van Lancker*	51
Rain *Cameron Versteeg*	52
Us Men *Eric Wiesemann*	53

2000 RIVER OF WORDS ART WINNERS   54

2000 River of Words GRAND PRIZE WINNER
Category I (Grades K-2)

Bugnibble

Wind blows,
Leaves fall.
Dead leaves hit the ground.
Bugs nibble holes
In the leaf's rattling carpet.

Calvin Hargis, Age 8
McCoy Elementary School
Aztec, New Mexico
Teacher: Diane Mittler

2000 RIVER OF WORDS GRAND PRIZE WINNER
Category II (Grades 3-6)

Swim In Me

swim in me
    i'm yours
        my waves
            yours
                my rivers
                    yours
                      my streams
                    yours
                my creeks
            yours
        my lakes
    yours
    my ponds
    yours
        my rain
            yours
                my clouds
              yours
            swim in me

            i'm yours

GRACIE JORDAN, Age 12
Nueva School
Hillsborough, California
Teacher: Carlo Cerruti

2000 RIVER OF WORDS GRAND PRIZE WINNER
Category III (Grades 7-9)

Rockefeller Wildlife Preserve: Mid-August

The air is moist
The water bittersweet
A southern Gulf breeze sighs
Laughing gulls call
And cicadas click their
Luminous song
I smell the death scent
Of beached gars
And see the dreamy haze
Of oil on water
Nearby an alligator stares
With tabby eyes
A great heron startles
From its marsh bed
Standing on the rip-rap,
I peer at the water
And slowly hoist
The turkey neck on string
A blue-point crab
Grips the bait
I slyly dip the net
A good two feet away
And scoop up the crustacean
Without warning
And drop it into a bucket
To meet many friends,
Gifts of the Mississippi,

The day has reached its climax
Animals sleep through the heat,
Hiding in the wax myrtles
A snowy egret,
White plumage glistening,
Glides into the Roseau cane.

KEVIN MAHER, Age 12
L.J. Alleman School
Lafayette, Louisiana
Teacher: Charles Mire

"Trees" by Angel Salto, Age 6, Brooklyn, New York, 2000 Category I Winner

2000 River of Words GRAND PRIZE WINNER
Category IV (Grades 10-12)

Dear Aquarius,

Tonight you bend
because the stars are fearless
enough to glow on you
They speak their truths in muted light
If one grain of sand is traced from a
twisting kiss in the North
to this forgiveness draped around my feet
then salvation lies in every loop and thrash
You keep your secrets well
in lengthy, passionate channels,
too gargling and gracefully
knitted to control
But Aquarius, I have
long held this view of you
basking in your semiprecious charm
When I was small, seven or so,
I'd put on brother's dingy jeans
and rill my way through silted grass,
to the steady saplings
blooming at your edge
Toe by toe, foot by dirtied foot
I disappeared
Everything from the mirror down
was me no more

KT Harmon, *Age 17*
All Saint's Episcopal School
Vicksburg, Mississippi
Teacher: Greg Sellers

2000 RIVER OF WORDS
INTERNATIONAL GRAND PRIZE WINNER

A flashing white fin appears,
Then vanishes
Into the muddy, light brown waters of the Yangtze River.
Unknown to human kind,
Before Three Gorges Dam began.
The dam in central China on the Yangtze River
Will produce much electricity
But will produce no good for this dolphin.

It swims upstream back to its birthplace on the same river,
To nurture its young,
Much like the salmon.
It cannot see,
But uses vibrations.
The most endangered dolphin in the world.
It will be wiped off the face of the earth
Within a few decades.

The Three Gorges Dam will block off the passage
which these dolphins swim through
to get to the nurturing ground.

The water was once filled with these quick creatures,
Streaks of white whenever you looked hard,
But now, threatened by the dam,
Fewer than 50 are left.
This soon-to-be-extinct dolphin only found in the Yangtze,
This white flash,
Flag bearer,
This dying creature,
Is, indeed,
The Baiji.

*Baiji in Mandarin means "the flag bearer that was left behind."

CHRISTINE YIN, *Age 13*
American International School of Guangzhou
Guangzhou, People's Republic of China
Teacher: Amy Shawver

2000 River of Words
ANACOSTIA WATERSHED PRIZE
(Honoring a Washington, DC Student)

Just Imagine

Just imagine
Waking up one day,
Looking out your window starting to say…

NO BAD SMELLS
NO SMOKE
NO NOISE
NO TRASH
NO CROWDED PLAYGROUNDS, BASKETBALL COURTS,
OR CORNERS LOADED WITH TEENS.
NO BAD WORDS ON THE WALLS AND SIDEWALKS
NO JUNK
NO MUDDY WATERS

NO HUNGER
NO POOR
NO PEER PRESSURE
NO ENVY
NO NAME CALLING

NO GUNS
NO FEAR
NO PAIN
NO MURDER
NO DRUGS

NO DEAD BIRDS BECAUSE OF
NO DEAD GRASS BECAUSE OF
NO DEAD TREES BECAUSE OF
NO DEAD PEOPLE BECAUSE OF
NO PLACE TO PLAY BECAUSE OF

CLEAN UP!
CARE!
HELP EACH OTHER!
PLAY!
GO OUTSIDE AND PLAY!
RUN!
SKIP!
JUMP!
RIDE!
SMILE!
BE HAPPY!
BE SAFE!
AND JUST IMAGINE BEING A KID
LIVING BY THE ANACOSTIA RIVER.

EL'JAY JOHNSON, Age 8
River Terrace Elementary School
Washington, DC
Teacher: Patricia Ann Goodnight

Nature's Notes

Rhythmic sounds of water
play out the notes of nature.
I hear it by the Sandbar Willow;
I see it seep up from
the red Earth,
to rustle
Fall's leftover leaves.
I feel it in the oak tree tunnel,
like a visit back through time,
where I see the parent tree
clone its first young.
I smell it on the muddy trails
where weasels, coyotes, and rabbits
have left their tracks behind.
I taste it within the air as
Mother Nature's child
and feel it in my bones, knowing
I can never be complete
without it.

AMY ALLRED, Age 18
Brighton High School
Salt Lake City, Utah
Teacher: Pat Russell

Snoqualmie River Flambé

Ingredients:
- Freshly melted snow from the spires of the Cascades
- Navy blue Blackberries as dark as the summer night's sky
- The stars and the planets mixed together in a pureé
- Marshmallowy clouds (in your reflection)
- Wild Mushrooms (you can find in any nearby heart of a forest; make sure that they are finely pounded by the sleek hooves of neighboring Elk)
- A black dog named Jazz (optional)
- About 100,000 acres of lush, green farmland

Directions:
1. Mix all of the ingredients together except for the clouds and the farmland.
2. After many moons stop stirring and let it sit for five days. Then soak in the finest silks from India and sprinkle across a dry landscape in Washington (whichever you choose).
3. Surround your river with the farmland and then wait until they connect.
4. Float the clouds up to the sky; wait until they have made themselves comfortable in heaven (they will add flavor to your reflection).
5. If you put the dog in your mixture then he would have not been mixed up with the others. He is probably swimming now in your river having the time of his life!
6. Take yourself on a walk in the misty morning; find yourself a comfortable spot on the bank of the river.

▼

Gaze into the river until you've found your reflection, have a nice conversation with him/her. Learn something special about yourself.

WARNING: NOTE THAT MANY HAVE BEEN TURNED INTO A NARCISSUS. BE CAREFUL.

ROBIN ANDREWS, Age 11
Lakeside Middle School
Seattle, Washington
Teacher: Alicia Hokanson

"Quick As My Thought" by Rachel Rees, Age 10, Susanville, California, 2000 Category II Winner

One with

The wind blows beneath my arms, wrapping
lovingly around me
I see the eyes of the untamed bobcat and see
myself untamed
I hear the songs of my ancestors and piece myself
together
I am one with my heart and know who I am

SABLE ARAGON, *Age 14*
J.E. Cosgriff Memorial School
Salt Lake City, Utah
Teacher: Mr. Baird

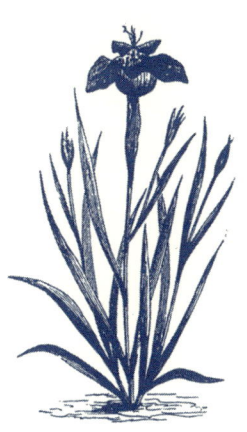

Eluding the Familiar

The eternal search for a signal haunts me.
An epiphany—something life altering—waits in the wings
to be awakened.

But I can't find the emptiness that thinking needs:
no place lacks connections—
a strong fishing line
reels me into the past.

I have yet to come across that refuge
where every thought isn't a memory,
and every memory doesn't drown me
in could haves and should haves.

Once upon a time doesn't intrigue me.
The present should offer enough,
but I can't seem to find my place here.

The color of the sea before a storm: grey;
the call of a cardinal: pure and high;
a morning spider web: keeper of the secrets of the universe.

All I know, I've known forever.

Anne Atwell-McLeod, Age 14
The Center for Teaching & Learning
Edgecomb, Maine
Teacher: Nancie Atwell

Water Shed Poem

Tread of pale stream,
Hemming watery licks.
And pebbles promise
Tootsie nooks
Burrowed scarce
Amongst the wind
And willow creep.
Finger tips,
Strain of sky,
Winged on ripping sun stripe.
Flight made on robin.
Torn in a scarlet
Slaughtered breast.
And moon bond leaves
Gilded in palms of dream brooks.

LUCY BARBER, Age 11
Denver School of the Arts
Denver, Colorado
Teacher: Jana Clark

In Memoriam

the deciduous nanny
governed and created order among the children who ran
in turn we made careful jewelry for her long willowy limbs
we sat on her lap pleading with her to tell us stories
about her roots
and the way things are

she always stood tall
protecting us from the snow and the rain
and everything outside that didn't delight us
even when her thick head of foliage began to thin

we cried when she disappeared
without warning without a funeral
we didn't know if she had been ill
or if she was murdered

or perhaps she decided
she'd had enough of this life
we never knew

in disbelief we turned away from her lonely remains
which seemed so cold and detached
and we remembered how she made us smile
we couldn't imagine she'd ever betray us
she was the tall upright beauty who had our love so fully
who we were sure would always be there
it all collapses finally
doesn't it?

nothing else was ever so good to dance around
no one ever understood us so well
she silently mothered all of us

that corner of our childhood world looks so empty now

ALEXIS KELLNER BECKER, Age 13
The Center for Teaching & Learning
Edgecomb, Maine
Teacher: Nancie Atwell

Twilight

Oh skies
of blue,
Cerulean shades,
Evening's painted beauty made
In artist's eye
flowing dark
Wisping crawl,
Whispering call
Of twilight glories shining

E.A. BLEVINS, Age 16
Hahnville High School
Boutte, Louisiana
Teacher: Colleen Winkler

The Rain

Dark
Pouring
Scary
Black
Puddle
Night

MADDISON BOEWE, Age 6
Pine Knob Elementary School
Clarkston, Michigan
Teacher: Beth Gifford

First Winter's Fog

The fog floats upon the fields
Blanketing each haybale, barn, animal—
Shrouding every object in its icy, cobwebbing
Mist.
The moon reflects upon the stilled waters
Of the slough, shining as bright
As in the sky, glowing with the stillness
Of the night.
Trees, bare from winter's cold,
Stand alone, silhouetted against the sky
Of evening, reaching, gesturing as the breeze stirs
Their freezing branches.
"On the night that you were born," Mom says,
"There was fog."
"Fog," you think,
"Fog."

MARGIT BOWLER, Age 10
John Jacob Astor Elementary School
Astoria, Oregon
Teacher: Tom Wilson

The Storm Is Coming

Wind whistles through
The pine needles twirl
Sawgrass sways
While clouds dash by

Little creatures hide
The pond waters splash
Rain gushes down
And tickles my toes

Kevin Brown, Age 5
Lake Park Baptist School
Lake Park, Florida
Teacher: Mrs. Long

Snow

Snow tumbling
in the dark of December,
in the silver,
shimmering,
black, cloudy sky.

Chris Castillo, Age 7
North Sashabaw Elementary School
Clarkston, Michigan
Teachers: Mrs. Skorupski / Mrs. Santola

Cool, fresh rain water,
Runs off aunty's umbrella,
Then makes a big splash.

Josh Coomber, *Age 7*
Whitehawk Primary School
Brighton, England
Teacher: John McKay

"Untitled" by Shintaro Maeda, Age 14, Wichita, Kansas, 2000 Category III Winner

Here is Life

Silvering drops of rain
Weep into a silent river
Wash over knowing stones
Fly over snarling rapids
Ripple through quiet ponds.
A mink rolls to the surface,
Disappears once more in a trail of rolling bubbles.

The storm quiets,
The sun returns from banishment.
A golden mist lifts wraithlike to join the milky monarchs of the sky,
Column clouds, heralding a storm
Somewhere else.
Invisible winds carry the lofty nimbuses to answer a desert's thirsty cry.
The elusive coyote shakes rainwater from his sandy fur
And the cliff rose blooms.

On the other extreme of life
There lies another desert,
A frozen world of snow and ice.
The northern lights play over water bound in the polar caps.
The hour of the lemming has come on the land
Soon the myriad furry creatures will render themselves to the sea.
The Arctic wolf rules the land and the gyrfalcon rules the air.

Over the ocean a black tempest reigns.
The clouds give fresh water back to the sea
And the salt engulfs it.

Soon the sun will appear
And create clouds in the stratosphere
To fly with the wind
To rain into a river
And fall on the mink.
Here is life.

>   **KELLY COX,** *Age 14*
>   *Home School / Cascade Middle School*
>   *Bend, Oregon*
>   *Teacher: Mr. Molner*

What a good looking piece of land with a lot of
Animals,
That is the way of nature.
Everything has its own place like the
Red Headed Woodpecker
Stabbing at the
Hardwoods with his
Elusive,
Dark beak.

>   **JOSH DAVIDSON,** *Age 11*
>   *Liberty Middle School*
>   *Ashland, Virginia*
>   *Teacher: Mrs. Tufaro*

Water

      Water of hope.
      Water of dream.
The bugs dance on it like little fairies.
The trees touch it with a silver magic wand.
      Water of spirit.
      Water of love.
The trickle of drops that look like little diamonds.
      Water of song.
      Water of heart.
The crickets sing like children.
The plants grow from the heart of the ground.
      Water of me.
      Water of you.
The way I tell the poem.
The way you listen.

Shawna Eiermann, Age 11
Cross and Crown Lutheran School
Rohnert Park, California
Teachers: Mrs. Hartnet / Mrs. Ridenour

The Storm is Here

The storm is here.
I know because the frogs have become an omnipresent force.
Their song engulfing me in a wave of monotonous music.
My hair is sopping with rainwater.
My hands are covered in the earth's brown glory.
The storm is here.
I know because the fog is solid.
Its fingers extending through the forest blinding those who rely on sight.
The weather begins to speak and I listen.
Taking in its magnificence through every orifice in my body.
The storm is here.
I know because the forest has grown deathly silent.
The leaves are restless I can see them sway with impatience.
The wind begins to gather force recruiting its power from the currents.
I can feel it all around me its voice telling the world to tremble.
The storm is here.

MILES FELD, Age 16
Tamalpais High School
Mill Valley, California
Teacher: Karen Benson

First Light

On that day, the first day, wise water,
heavy with our dreams
carries deep into the glen over rocks and through trees
until it reaches a dam.
And there standing on that dam shall be one man,
grown old and fat,
the man who betrayed the sun and moon.
He is standing, floating above the sick, dying river.
Behind him the water masses in a great rush.
Then, on that day the water will push
at the skeleton hands of cement until at last they
break before the water's wrath.
Then the water will rush free away from the man
and the broken remains of the dam.
The day shall rise with the sun and beauty will return to the land.
Water will flow again
and wonder will be seen glistening
as first light sparkles on the free water.

GRAHAM FISCHER-CORNERS, Age 16
Denver School for the Arts
Denver, Colorado
Teacher: Jana Clark

Goldfish

Clear flowing
  Water
    Rushes down
      Stream
        As tiny
          Glazing
          Goldfish scatter
        To
      Their mother
    Like
  Lightning.

Stefani Galik, Age 8
North Sashabaw Elementary
Clarkston, Michigan
Teacher: Mrs. Pitser

Mariquita

Escondida entre las ramas
Me pregunto, ¿cómo te llamas?

Mariquita te llamaré
Y en mis manos te tomaré

Te soltaré y volarás
Y mi deseo cumplirás

Ladybug

Hidden between the branches
I ask myself, what's your name?

Ladybug I will name you
and in my hands I will take you

I will free you and let you fly
And you will make my wish come true

YUTZEL GARCIA, Age 9
Anderson Valley Elementary School
Boonville, California
Teacher: Julie Rumble

a
single
drop

a
single
drop of crystal
suspended in time
for a golden moment
caught in the glinting light of
the sun a miniature rainbow
landscape of flowing colors
merging into a pool of molten
lava that glistens reflecting the
beauty of the outside world in a
minuscule looking glass that is
invaluable to the joy of

puddle jumping
children

EMILY SMITH GILBERT, *Age 13*
South Meadow School
Peterborough, New Hampshire
Teacher: Mrs. Morash

Moon Song

All night long, I danced with the moon
My bare feet soared over the forest floor
As I blew kisses to the trees
I plunged my hands into the icy depths
Of a new summer spring
And felt a shiver of delight rise in me
I slipped my feet into the shining sky
Reflected in the swaying pool
A sigh seeps from my lips
And I lean against a tree to dream
Now that I am seasons older, I still dream with trees
But not as long
I still share secrets with new summer springs
But not as many
I still blow kisses to the trees
But not as much
My feet still soar over the forest floor
But not as high
And I still dance with the moon
But not as quick.

ALICE GOLDFUSS, Age 12
Chenango Bridge Elementary School
Binghamton, New York
Teacher: Mrs. Pierce

The Secret of the River

Running through the meadows,
While the wind blows in my hair.
I hurry to the river.
There is a secret there.

As I near the rushing waters,
I hear the cooing doves.
I sit beside my river,
and watch the clouds above.

On the mountains in the distance,
The pine trees touch the sky.
I listen to my river,
and let the world go by.

The secret of the river
Is peace and joy and rest.
Gazing at the heavens,
I know that I am blessed.

JOANNA LAINE ISAACS, Age 12
Covenant School (Home School)
Boone, North Carolina
Teacher: Carol Isaacs

Virga

Sky stretched tight
over hard dry land
The rivers are ribbons of silky dust
Snaking arroyos
tangled lengths of abandoned beds
where rocks cannot be smoothed
by the smooth steady rush

Clouds pass hurriedly by
refusing the smallest breath of moisture
bearing their gifts eleswhere
While the sun returns to beat down
upon a landscape it has thoroughly tamed
Wind whistles through, sparkling
as freshness is borne to regions afar

Now it is an afternoon in August
the sky a palette of unreal blues and greys
Clouds here for a short stay only
tear suddenly open at their swollen seams
and the rain begins to fall
It evaporates briskly above the horizon
but soon violent drops raise the sulky dust

Narrow canyon beds rush swollen with water
Pounding forward like the sound of blood in your ears
exuberantly destructive for a few short moments
before the sun shreds the velvet clouds
before the earth sucks the damp greedily away
The sky gazes blankly, inexpressive
and the desert settles in to wait

> **MALLORY A. JENSEN,** *Age 16*
> *Santa Fe Preparatory School*
> *Santa Fe, New Mexico*
> *Teacher: Rob Wilder*

"Untitled" by Eon Hatter, Age 15, Decatur, Georgia, 2000 Category IV Winner

The Late Rose

It curls by the gate, biding its time.
Spring is gone, and Summer is waning.
Autumn? A hairsbreadth away.

The breeze sweeps on,
Swinging the gate on its rusty hinges,
Gently filtering through the sun-hued bud.

Creamy pink deep within,
Petals the color of the sunset sky,
Tinged with gold.

My eyes trace the path of your
Slender stalk, saw-edged leaves
Whispering quietly to Zephyrus.

The last fresh petal unfolds,
The silk-smooth skin of secret treasures
Spilling perfume into the woods.

Four days of full-fledged glory,
The moaning wind
Spills your beauty on the soil.

As crimson leaves crunch.

I tread softly, knowing
That you will have another year to rest,
And I will have another year to wait.

Jane S. Jiang, Age 11
Lakeside Middle School
Seattle, Washington
Teacher: Alicia Hokanson

The River

Whispering as she flows over pebbles
Gurgling with glee over rocks
Chattering excitedly through boulders and logs
Roaring at the top of her lungs
As she sails over a waterfall
Growing swifter as she widens
Her mouth opens as she beholds
The wondrous sight of the ocean.

JOHN KEOUGH, Age 13
South Meadow School
Peterborough, New Hampshire
Teacher: Mrs. Morash

Berry Falls

Spraying sounds of crashing water   speeding over slick,
         mossy rocks seep
             into my ears. Flittering droplets
     tickle my   face and
I can almost taste   the calm.

MALCOLM KIM, Age 10
Nueva School
Hillsborough, California
Teacher: Carlo Cerruti

The Air

The air is swift,
the air is strong.
It drags me
across the shimmering
floor of one lonely world.
Icicles glimmer in the sunshine.
Red berries fall
from bare trees.
The wind has swept the
leaves off the trees.
Bare trees shiver.

EMILY KIRBY, Age 7
North Sashabaw Elementary
Clarkston, Michigan
Teachers: Mrs. Santola / Mrs. Skorupski

Poseidon in the Infirmary

Cold water
lying still between cement walls
a river once, I guess,
but now you barely move
content to sleep
in peace and silence.
Your watery eyes
once so clear and blue
have fogged now,
grown brown,
clouded with dirt and algae
and your skin is covered with wrinkles—
ripples—
lazy in the breeze.
In your youth you were
a river
an ocean
a thunderstorm
you were Poseidon.
But lying here now,
in the grey concrete bunker,
you are dying.
Old and infirm, the strength you had
to rush, to fall, to crush
is gone
and you are left with age
and the wet wool smell
of dead water.

ANAÏS KOIVISTO, Age 15
San Francisco School of the Arts
San Francisco, California
Teacher: Heather Woodward

Wood of Feeling

Bark of cinnamon
Streams of laughter
Rain of cold
Seeds of soft and silky
Smell of warm
Drop of blue
Dew of misty
Wind of beauty
Wood of feeling

HANNAH MEADE, Age 9
Linscott Charter School
Watsonville, California
Teachers: Karen Mora / Linda Cover

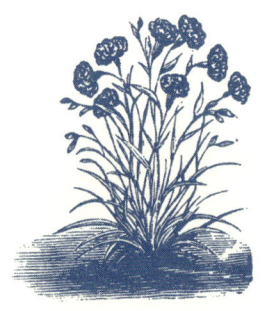

Deep Song of the River

O frabjous river of sweet water!

Up on Elk Mountain at summer's end,
The wild Gallinas rushes, gushes over stone.

White tail deer race along the bank.

You can hear jays chatter in the blue spruce,
See squirrels gather acorns to hide in soft soil.

Brown bears come fish, stock up on rainbow and German browns,
Oak leaves like orange butterflies, flutter to the still-warm ground.

When winter comes, the snow will fall,

The forest choir grows silent,
Then you hear
the secret, icy music of river.

       Mod 1 Class Poem (Collaborative)
       Memorial Middle School
       Las Vegas, New Mexico
       Teachers: Patti Olsen / Judyth Hill

Wonder of Wonders

Under a raindrop,
under a stream,
under a snowflake,
under a dream.
All the things you wish to do
in this land all come true.

Ian Olsen, Age 9
Lincoln Elementary School
Independence, Kansas
Teacher: Mrs. King

"Untitled" by Brett Docherty, Age 17, Mill Valley, California, Shasta Bioregion Prize

Sunset

As God falls asleep,
the roaring fire of orange and yellow in his eye
simmers down
to a single flicker
of brilliant purples and blues.

The flowers draw up their blankets
and the river gently massages
the rocks
to rest.

Then the raven spreads a protective wing
over the world,
and her golden eye
watches over us,
as she sings a stale song
of the dying day.

DAPHNE PAYNE, Age 13
Minnehaha Academy
Minneapolis, Minnesota
Teacher: Judy Hinck

Do You Hear It?

The ocean is breathing, do you hear it?
Its soft breaths roll with every wave
They crash upon the sandy beach
Making their mark upon the shore

The ocean is whispering, do you hear it?
Its soft voice is a melody of the wind across the water.
It whistles silently through our minds
Making its mark upon our souls

The ocean is calling, do you hear it?
The sweet sound of life beneath
It calls to you, it calls to me
Making its mark upon our hearts

The ocean is weeping, do you hear it?
The silent cries rise from the deep
Its pleading for us to save it
Making its mark upon our conscience

Will you help it? Do you hear it?
The voice so sweet, and gentle
All it asks is that you help
And keep its breaths safe from harm

Tiffany Pope, Age 16
Granby High School
Norfolk, Virginia
Teacher: Nadine Hook

Woods Canyon Lake

Back in the days of piggy-back rides,
When a young man carried a child,
Favorite memories were unknowingly formed
On the icy surface of Woods Canyon Lake.

Wrapped in denim and wool,
Cushioned by the heat of the white winter sun,
Snow angels grabbing hold
And forever embracing.

One hole scratched through a sheet of ice,
Two gathered, peering into a sea of fish,
Gentle bites, excited, quiet movements.
The piggy-back ride home a little bit heavier.

Beth Prall, Age 17
North High School
Phoenix, Arizona
Teacher: Marily Buehler

The Rhythm of Life

The ground beneath us is our past
The air above is our future.

The earth is our mother
Time is our father.

Mother Earth does not belong to us
We belong to the earth.

Man did not weave the web of life
He is just a tiny strand in it.

ALICIA D. PURDIN, Age 17
Gordon Central High School
Calhoun, Georgia
Teacher: Joan Graham

The Millionth Circle

Rippling outward
In
twinkling vibrations
Flickering under the silent
Orb of the moon
The stars giddy
With the sight of countless circles
The fish smile
A mere kiss can cause
a million circles

Leia Sandmann, Age 12
GreenWood School
Mill Valley, California
Teacher: Devika Brandt

Mother of the Earth

The river stretches her arms around the earth embracing it with care.
She gently shapes it over time,
And quenches its thirst when it is dry.
She feeds it with the plants and animals she carries.
The sound of her bubbling voice rocks it to sleep.
The river is like a mother to the Earth.

>   *CHRISTIE SWANSON, Age 14*
>   *Goddard Middle School*
>   *Littleton, Colorado*
>   *Teacher: Mary Ratigan*

Elements

Sometimes a beautiful field
follows me home in my mind
And I get the impression
that it was there for me
that it has been waiting
and the stalks whisper
giddy secrets and I know
that eternity rests in these grasses
so much so that
its wisdom sighs in rippling gusts
that buffet my mind
in bursts of recognition
and I am freed
Like so many seeds to the wind
I am spiraling downwards
until I realize that

Embers are stoked
rising out of the darkness
to become known all too well
and they burn like my mind
almost as truly on fire
and just as deeply destructive
I am enraged by the darkness
fighting it with licking blows
that forever stretch skywards
forever trying to illuminate
those mysterious black heavens
and I am freed
because even the heavens are
filled with fire
the time has arrived

The oceans travel farther
than you and I can dream
yet they remain inside themselves
sipping at worldly sands
with unspecific and smooth fingers
gurgling playful questions
that lull us to sleep
just before we grasp the answers
and the water doesn't mind
if we float or if we sink
as long as we keep swimming
surging along like so many rivers
and I am freed
drinking my fill of the world
and quenched by the water
for the rivers run deep and

I have become one
surging with strength
that runs at me from forgotten shadows
I have awakened from death and am fully alive
chasing the breezes at the crossroads
where past   present   and my future meet and shake hands
I have surrendered to my passion
Deeply in love with all the senses
so that each throbbing star makes me shudder
when it pulses in time to the galaxies
and each sun spattered flower
smiles as I dance in oblivion
for only I hear the music in my head
and only I am sure that I have kissed this one moment
so let the dawn break
and I'll stand firm as it shatters into rose tinted shards at my feet

Marla Scott, Age 17
Cedar Shoals High School
Athens, Georgia
Teacher: Dr. McWhorter

Shrimping

Laughter on the water, at the dock, cast and pull,
music of water and voices.
Salt water in the mouth, taste the river mud.
Reach for the net, arm goes down, hold with your teeth, cast, spin,
and release.
Breathe.
Crash of water. Spray on the wind.

Hand over hand, cast and pull,
laughter at a caught fish, a squid. Stop to watch a heron.
Missed throw, the net twists.
Crash, pull it in, and throw again.
Laughter as a ten-year-old boy tries to throw a fifty-pound net.
Catch him before he goes in.

Sun goes down in the marsh. Light the lamps.
Crickets sing and moonlight reflects off the water.
Moths hum and bump at the lights, shrimp till the tide changes.

Orange fades to blue, night sky. Night on the marsh, the river.
Sit and watch the tide.
Birds cry, marsh smell of salt and water, marsh mud and wood smoke.
Pine bugs whir and scream in the dark. Lap of water on the dock.
Tired voices murmur, soft laughter.
A cool breeze whips wet and tired faces.
Cools the body and the mind.

Pack up the nets; blow out the lamps, head home.
Sit in the kitchen and clean shrimp.
Get kicked out of the kitchen and sit on the porch and clean shrimp.
Pick up by the antenna, pinch off the head.

Old men drinking beer and telling stories.
Flash of cigarettes in the dark, sweet smoke.
Glow of charcoal, hamburgers on the grill.
Old women in the kitchen cracking jokes, laughter as they cook.
Crabs on the stove, coleslaw on the counter, peanuts on the boil.
Life, the river.

AMELIA SIDES, Age 18
A.R. Johnson High School
Augusta, Georgia
Teacher: Audrey Smith

The Clouds Are Once Again Too Big

I once dreamt I was a fisherman,
fearless and untouchable
casting from dusk 'til dawn,
catching the largest red snapper
known to man.
I was on an expedition in the Galapagos.
An open plain stretched for miles
to a ledge overlooking
a waterfall, its crystal blue
freeness gleaming in the sun.
And when night fell,
ebony water wept with the moon.
A whistle of silence
blew over the whitecaps.
I found myself
once more, a fisherman
out to sea. The clouds
overwhelmed with a power I wish I had,
to see as they do, all that
they control. Instead, I drift on,
held captive in a net of blue embrace.

Lyndsey Turner, Age 16
All Saint's Episcopal School
Vicksburg, Mississippi
Teacher: Greg Sellers

Tide

The waves gently stroke the sand,
then pull away discreetly,
as if I had done something
to offend their presence.

Gusts

The blue-green breeze slips in
through a crack in the window.
Billowing the white curtain
like a sail at sea.

HANS VAN LANCKER, Age 15
Martin County High School
Stuart, Florida
Teacher: Ms. Williams

Rain

The rain comes
gently to my face.

The landscape
screams color.

A thoughtful walk,
a touch, a kiss.

Soul and earth:
purified.

CAMERON VERSTEEG, *Age 13*
J.E. Cosgriff School
Salt Lake City, Utah
Teacher: Jeff Baird

Us Men

waterproofed to the waist,
see a vision, that to us
only comes once a year.
We are grumbling, stalking
out to the shed, to the purr
of engines warming.
Our breath spirits the chilled wind.
All day, work.
For the first time I am a part of it,
deserving of the reward that will come.
We sink back into cold metal bunkers
dug along gumbo levees
the color of potter's clay.
Dried stalks & weeds sway as cover.
In the distance, floodwater
rises against the sunburst ray
of a dying day. I hear the geese faintly
honk & gaggle above me. I see silhouettes
dot the horizon. There are splashes
of touch & go, wings flapping.
Yes, I do hope they like it here.
My father reaches for his boy,
                              and I give in.

ERIC WIESEMANN, Age 15
All Saint's Episcopal School
Vicksburg, Mississippi
Teacher: Greg Sellers

2000 RIVER OF WORDS ART WINNERS

GRAND PRIZE WINNERS

Category I (Grades K-2)
Angel Salto, Age 6
Brooklyn, New York
PS 23Q
Teacher: Mr. Goldstein

Category II (Grades 3-6)
Rachel Rees, Age 10
Susanville, California
Submitted independently
Teacher: Petra Rees

Category III (Grades 7-9)
Shintaro Maeda, Age 14
Wichita, Kansas
Wichita High School East
Teacher: Jennifer Fry

Category IV (Grades 10-12)
Eon Hatter, Age 15
Decatur, Georgia
Avondale Estates High School
Teacher: Pamela Segers (2000 ROW Teacher of the Year)

Shasta Bioregion Prize (Honoring a SF Bay Area Student)
Brett Docherty, Age 17
Mill Valley, California
Tamalpais High School
Teacher: Karen Benson

FINALISTS

ALEXEI ANISIN, Age 10, Novato, California
JULIYA BACHUR, Age 13, Chernyachov, Ukraine
ANDREW BERNAL, Age 17, Las Cruces, New Mexico
ERICK BROWN, Age 16, Stone Mountain, Georgia
BRANDON CARTER, Age 18, Atlanta, Georgia
EVA COVER, Age 8, Watsonville, California
CHRISTIAN FERNANDES, Age 10, Hopatcong, New Jersey
NATALIE HAMILL, Age 17, Princeton, New Jersey
MOLLY JESSUP, Age 10, Santa Ynez, California
ROBIN MIRANDA, Age 9, Santa Cruz, California
COURTNEY MCCUTCHEN, Age 17, Avondale Estates, Georgia
EMILY NEWDOW, Age 17, Atlanta, Georgia
KRISTINA RIDDLE, Age 12, Kalispell, Montana
CHARITY SCOTT, Age 16, Baltimore, Maryland
WHITNEY WHEELER, Age 11, Crawford, Georgia

2000 RIVER OF WORDS TEACHER OF THE YEAR
PAMELA SEGERS
Avondale Estates High School
Decatur, Georgia

TO VIEW THE WINNERS' ARTWORK
Please visit our site on the Internet:
www.riverofwords.org